The Gruesome Truth About

The
Romans

Written by

Jillian Powell

Illustrated by

Matt Buckingham

WAYLAND

First published in 2008 by Wayland

Text copyright © Wayland 2008
Illustration copyright © Matt Buckingham 2008

Wayland
338 Euston Road
London NW1 3BH

Wayland Australia
Level 17/207 Kent Street
Sydney NSW 2000

Senior Editor: Claire Shanahan
Design Manager: Paul Cherrill
Designers: Fiona Grant, Jason Billin
Consultant: Anne Millard
Indexer: Cath Senker

British Library Cataloguing in Publication Data
Powell, Jillian
The gruesome truth about the Romans
1. Rome - Social life and customs - Juvenile literature
2. Rome - History - Juvenile literature
I. Title II. The Romans 937

ISBN 978 0 7502 5336 9

Printed in China

Wayland is a division of Hachette Children's Books,
an Hachette Livre UK company.
www.hachettelivre.co.uk

Contents

The Super Romans

Rome was one of the world's first superpowers.

The Romans lived in Italy over 2,000 years ago, from around 500 BCE to 400 CE. Rome was a city state that grew to rule a great empire of 60 million people. It owned lands stretching from the Mediterranean to North Africa and the Middle East. The Romans had powerful leaders, strong laws, spectacular theatres and public games.

The Romans were great engineers...

◄ ...who built triumphal arches...

◄ ...grand arenas...

▲ ...and impressive aqueducts for clean water.

How Rome was made

There is a legend that Rome was founded by the brothers Romulus and Remus in 753 BCE.

►Their wicked uncle threw the babies into the River Tiber...

Gruesome truth

Those are some things that you probably already know about the Romans, but in this book you'll find out the gory and grisly bits that no one ever tells you! Each double page will begin with a well-known FACT, before going on to tell you the **gruesome truth**. Look out for these features throughout the book – the answers are on page 32.

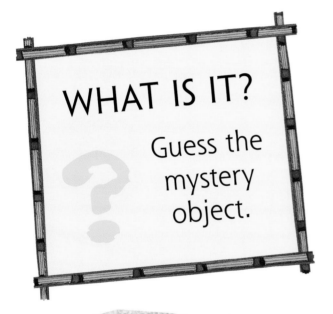

WHAT IS IT?

Guess the mystery object.

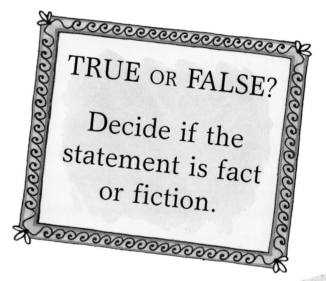

TRUE OR FALSE?

Decide if the statement is fact or fiction.

▼ When they grew up, they killed their uncle and built a city on the banks of the Tiber. But one day, they argued and, in a fight, Romulus killed Remus, so the city was named after him.

▲ But they were found and raised by a she-wolf and later a shepherd.

Blood and Guts

FACT The Romans built grand arenas like the **Colosseum** in Rome, which could seat 50,000 spectators. Emperors and rich Romans paid for the shows and the crowds had free entertainment.

Gruesome truth

The crowds came to see people and animals killing each other. Most men who died in the Colosseum were 18 to 25 years old.

Arena stars

Gladiators were trained fighters. They were usually slaves captured in war. The best gladiators were celebrities, a bit like today's football stars. Some were famous for fighting wild animals. Others fought wearing blindfolds!

Crowd control

Criminals were also thrown into the ring to fight. When a man became injured or exhausted, the crowd yelled at the emperor to save or kill him.

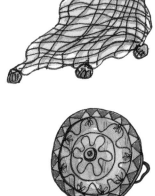

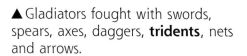

▲ Gladiators fought with swords, spears, axes, daggers, **tridents**, nets and arrows.

If the emperor decided the man should die, two men would then come on, one wearing a winged helmet, the other a hawk mask. The first struck the criminal with a red-hot poker. The other hit him on the head with a hammer. His dead body was then hooked and dragged off stage as the crowd roared with excitement.

WHAT IS IT?

TRUE OR FALSE?

If the emperor gave the thumbs up, the man was saved.

▲ The arena's floor was covered in sand to soak up all the blood. It had trap doors and lifts leading to cages where men and animals were kept.

Thrills, Spills, Kills

FACT The Romans loved a day at the races.

Gruesome truth

Chariot racing often ended in spectacular crashes and injury or death on the racetrack.

The greatest circus

The Circus Maximus (meaning 'greatest circus' in Latin) was bigger than any super stadium today. It could seat 250,000 spectators. Twelve chariots with either two or four horses raced each other around the track at high speed. They often crashed, losing wheels and injuring or killing the drivers.

Teams and tablets

There were four teams: the Reds, Greens, Blues and Whites. Violence sometimes broke out between rival fans.

People often took bets on the winning teams. Some buried curse tablets at the racetrack, wishing injury or death on to one of the charioteers, so their team would win!

Headless horses

When a horse won a race, it was sometime killed as a sacrifice to Mars, the god of war, and its head was displayed on a wall.

Roman boxing

The Romans also enjoyed boxing matches. Instead of padded gloves, the boxers wore leather bands with deadly spikes in them to pack a bloody punch.

WHAT IS IT?

▼ Studs and spikes on gloves left some boxers crippled for life.

▶ Boys stood by the tracks throwing water onto the chariot wheels to cool them down. Sometimes they were swept up and killed, too.

▲ The first driver to complete seven laps of the stadium was the winner.

9

Deadly Arts

FACT The Romans loved theatre.

Gruesome truth

The audiences sometimes watched condemned criminals being killed for real on stage.

Slaves and stunts

Most plays were staged in open-air theatres. Sometimes, people spent all day at the theatre, watching different shows such as comedies, tragedies, **farces** and pantomimes.

The audience sometimes walked out if the play was not violent enough. They enjoyed watching torture and even death. The actors were often slaves, but criminals were brought on to do stunts. Sometimes, they had to fight to the death with a bear or dress in golden clothes and dance on stage before their clothes were set on fire.

Bones and bladders

Gambling with dice was popular. The Romans also played ball games using balls made from pigs' bladders or cats' guts.

▼ The Romans played a game called 'knuckle bones' using the ankle bones of sheep or goats.

▲ Handball was played as well as kinds of football and hockey.

▼ Roman actors were booed, pelted with apples or given a beating if the audience didn't like them.

Art attack

The Romans were skilled at making mosaics, glass and pottery. They didn't all have pretty decorations. Some show scenes of criminals tied to posts being savaged by lions or tigers.

◄ Many Roman vases show gladiators fighting wild animals.

11

Hygiene and Hair

FACT The Romans had toilets, toothpaste and hair gel.

Gruesome truth

Most Romans used public toilets where you sat on seats in rows. Some toilets were open to view from the **forum**!

▼ There was no toilet paper, just a sponge on a stick that everyone shared. They rinsed it in a trough of water.

Useful urine
People also weed into big pots standing on street corners. The urine was collected and stored for several weeks. **Fullers** then used it for cleaning grease and dirt off clothes. It worked like bleach to whiten togas.

▶ Fullers came to empty the pots when they were full.

Disgusting dentistry

Rich Romans had slaves to clean their teeth. They used toothpicks and toothpaste made from crushed animal bones, horns or shells, mixed with urine. Sometimes, tree bark was added to improve the flavour!

Rotten teeth were filled with ash from mouse dung, dried whale flesh or lizards' livers.

▲ One remedy for bad teeth was boiling up earthworms and pouring the mixture into the ear.

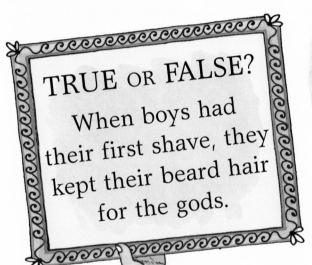

TRUE OR FALSE?

When boys had their first shave, they kept their beard hair for the gods.

Cloths and cobwebs

Most people shared public baths. Instead of soap, they used olive oil that was scraped off the body by slaves using metal **strigils**.

The Romans used hair gel made from goats' fat and beech wood ashes. If they had pimples, they covered them up with cloth patches. One remedy for shaving cuts was cobwebs soaked in vinegar.

◀ Body hair was removed with tweezers, **pumice stone** or hair removers made from **resin**, bats' blood and powdered snake.

Dormice and Bird Brains

FACT The Romans gave splendid dinner parties.

Gruesome truth

The Romans ate songbirds, ostrich brains and sows' udders.

Table manners
Slaves served guests who lay on couches to eat. Guests brought their own napkins and carried leftover food home in them. It was polite to burp.

During the meal, some guests went into a room where they made themselves sick so they could eat more.

▲ Another Roman delicacy was dormouse.

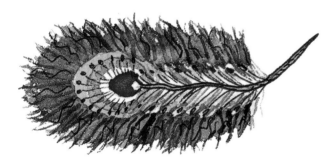

◄ The Romans used perfumed feathers to tickle their throats and make themselves sick.

Mouldy meals
Garum was a popular cooking sauce made from fish guts. It was sometimes used to flavour and disguise the taste of rotten meat or fish. One gourmet dish was licker fish, which fed on sewage in the River Tiber.

▲ Experts have discovered that the Romans ate rotten meat and fish by examining their sewage!

▼ Some emperors were famous **gluttons**. Maximilian is said to have got through 20 kilograms of meat and 34 litres of wine in a day.

Main course
Baked flamingo
Honey-roasted dormice
Snails fattened in milk
Peacocks' brains
Larks' tongues
Camels' heels

Gifts for the Gods

FACT The Romans were a religious people, who worshipped their gods at household shrines and city temples.

Gruesome truth

The Romans sacrificed people and animals as offerings to their gods.

Dangerous deities

The Romans believed that angry gods caused troubles like war, storms and disease. They tried to please the gods by making offerings of coins, statues, food and incense.

Animal offerings

Priests sacrificed animals at altars outside the temples. They killed everything from a single chicken to a herd of cattle. They used axes and knives to slaughter the animals, then collected the blood and splashed it over statues of the gods. The priests cut the animals open and removed their organs so they could study them for signs of the gods' will.

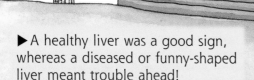

▶A healthy liver was a good sign, whereas a diseased or funny-shaped liver meant trouble ahead!

Skulls and superstitions

In parts of the empire, including Britain, the Romans sacrificed criminals, prisoners of war, even babies and old women. They practised head hunting as they thought taking an enemy's head gave them his power.

▼ Heads were thrown into wells, rivers or streams as offerings to the gods.

The Romans had many superstitions. They believed chickens were sacred and so watched the way they ate to try and tell the future. If they weren't eating, it was a bad day to travel or get married!

◀ Chickens and birds were thought to foretell the future.

WHAT IS IT?

POYEPAKLE VS.GNAVX

◀ Women believed combing their hair with the spear of a freshly killed gladiator would bring luck!

Crime and Punishment

FACT The Romans had strict laws and punishments for criminals.

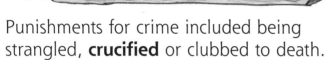

Gruesome truth

Punishments for crime included being strangled, **crucified** or clubbed to death.

A sacking offence!

The Romans believed that the punishment should fit the crime. If the crime was **arson**, the criminal was whipped, then set on fire.

Being 'sacked' meant being sewn into a leather sack and thrown into a river. This was a punishment that the Emperor Claudius liked to watch. It was used for crimes like killing your father.

▲ If someone stole a deer, they wrapped them in the deer's skin and set hunting dogs loose on them!

▲ Often, something else like a snake, a dog, an ape or a cockerel was put in the sack, so that it would bite or peck the criminal as they drowned together.

Savage sentences

Traitors to Rome were beheaded. Their heads were tossed in the sewers and their bodies thrown in the River Tiber.

▼ For stealing food, criminals were sent to work in the mines.

◄ If they told lies in court, they were thrown off a high cliff, or if they **slandered** someone, they were clubbed to death.

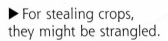
► For stealing crops, they might be strangled.

▼ Some criminals were tied to posts in the Colosseum and had wild animals set on them, usually for the lunch-time show!

Bloody Battles

FACT The Romans had a powerful and well-trained army.

Gruesome truth

Thousands of Roman soldiers died in battle, as well as civilians and prisoners of war from enemy countries.

Prisoner parades

Soldiers paraded prisoners of war in Rome before killing them in the city centre. Under the Emperor Trajan (98 – 117 CE), the army practised head hunting. They offered the heads of their enemies as a sacrifice to the gods of war.

▶ Crowds often gathered in the streets to watch prisoners being paraded and then killed.

Fighting talk

The Roman army could kill as many as 80,000 people in battle, mostly by stabbing or slashing using javelins and swords.

▼ Giant catapults called **ballistas** fired huge rocks weighing up to 45 kilograms.

◀ The Roman army often used their shields in a 'tortoise formation' to protect themselves.

Brandings and beatings

Discipline in the army was strict. Anyone who tried to avoid service was sentenced to death. New recruits were tattooed and branded to stop them deserting. The punishment for lazy behaviour was flogging. If a soldier ran away, he was beaten or stoned to death.

In 214 CE, 370 soldiers were thrown off the Tarpeian Rock in Rome for deserting. One general had deserters trampled to death by elephants.

▼ Tattoos stopped soldiers deserting by making them immediately recognisable as army men.

One in ten

The punishment for cowardly behaviour was **decimation**. This meant the **cohort** was lined up and one man in ten was clubbed to death. The survivors were fed on barley and had to sleep outside the camp in disgrace.

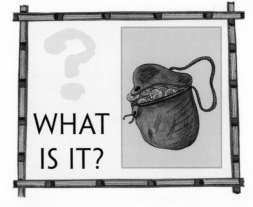

WHAT IS IT?

Masters and Slaves

FACT Roman slaves included doctors, dentists, actors, dancers and teachers.

Gruesome truth

Millions of slaves had no rights. Some masters thought of their slaves as 'tame animals' and beat them to punish them.

Cheap labour

Some people were born into slave families. Others were taken as prisoners, then sold in slave markets. A household slave cost around 500 **denarii**: that was cheaper than a horse or a cow! Some rich Romans owned hundreds of slaves.

▶ Slaves were often sold in chains, and had their heads shaved and their foreheads branded.

Working lives

Some slaves were trained as gladiators. Others worked for rich masters or mistresses. The slaves did all the cooking, cleaning and washing in Roman households.

▲ Slaves had to carry their masters and mistresses around the city in **litters**.

The cost of freedom

Some slaves could buy their freedom or win it as a famous gladiator. But many got their freedom granted only when their master died.

TRUE OR FALSE?

Slaves could be crucified for rebellion.

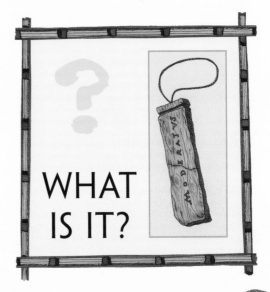

WHAT IS IT?

Medicine Men

FACT Roman **forts** had hospitals where surgeons carried out emergency operations on wounded soldiers.

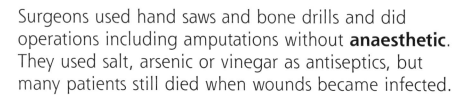

Gruesome truth

Surgeons used hand saws and bone drills and did operations including amputations without **anaesthetic**. They used salt, arsenic or vinegar as antiseptics, but many patients still died when wounds became infected.

▶ The acid in vinegar would sting on open wounds!

Quack remedies

Many people believed that diseases were caused by the gods, witchcraft or curses. Remedies included frogs cooked in olive oil to cure a fever, and drinking gladiators' blood to treat epilepsy.

Funny smells

Roman doctors believed the body was made up of four **humours**, which had to be kept in balance. They smelled a patient's sweat, spit, wee or vomit to check for signs of trouble. They often tried to cure illnesses using **leeches** or hot cups to draw out the patient's 'bad blood'.

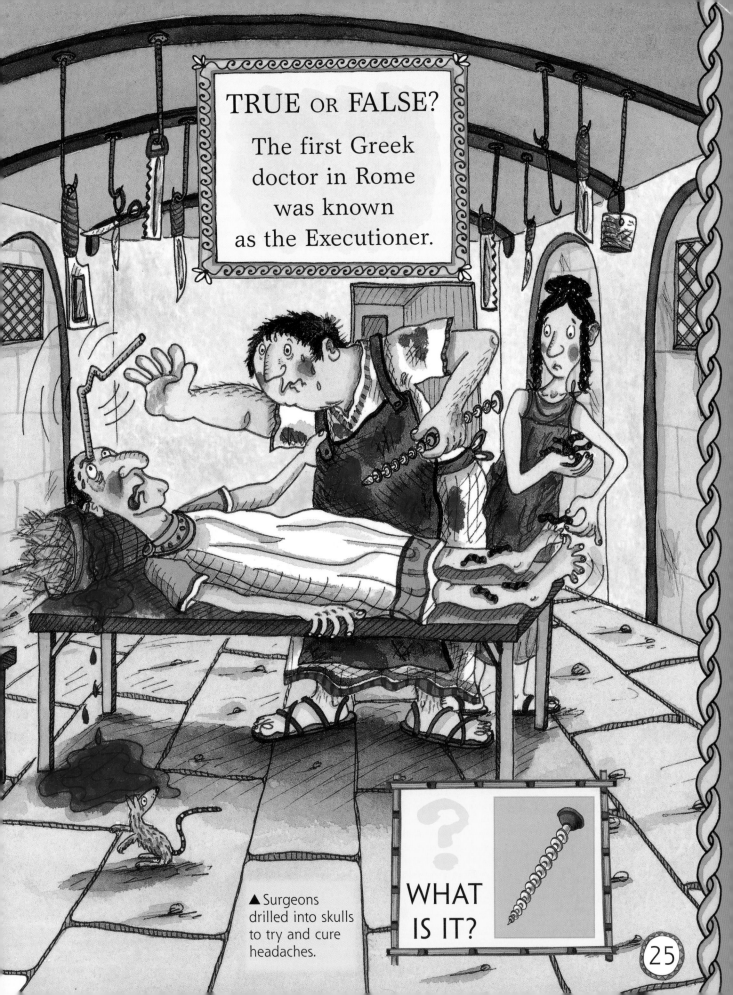

TRUE OR FALSE?

The first Greek doctor in Rome was known as the Executioner.

▲ Surgeons drilled into skulls to try and cure headaches.

WHAT IS IT?

Families and Funerals

FACT Family was very important to the Romans.

Gruesome truth

Roman fathers had the power of life or death over their family. A Roman father was head of the family, called the **pater familias**.

▼ The pater familias could arrange his children's marriages...

▲ ...sell them as slaves...

▶ ...and even claim their property.

Births and deaths

About one in three babies died as infants. Sometimes, they were plunged in cold water or left outside to see if they were strong enough to survive. If they were unwanted or the family could not afford to keep them, babies were drowned or left on the city rubbish dump. Sometimes, they were found by others and brought up as slaves. The remains of nearly 100 newborn babies were found near a villa in Roman Britain.

▲ Unwanted babies were often abandoned on hillsides.

Hard labour

The rich and poor lived very different lives. Many of the poor spent long hours working in the fields or in workshops.

▼ It was mostly boys from rich families who went to school. If they misbehaved, their classmates had to hold them down while they were given a whipping. Slaves and children of the poor were sent out to work.

Funeral fun

When Romans died, most were **cremated** but if buried, their graves were outside the city walls. Sometimes, they were buried face down, or their head was cut off and placed at their feet. At family funerals, some people hired clowns and dancers, and often they told jokes about the dead person or made fun of them.

▼ Professional mourners were paid to wail and cry at funerals.

27

Evil Emperors

FACT Roman emperors ruled over a mighty empire for 400 years.

Gruesome truth

Some emperors were famous for their cruelty. They killed anyone who went against them, even their own family.

Victory parades

When the army won important battles, the Emperor led a victory parade through Rome. He rode in a gold chariot with his soldiers, their prisoners and treasures they had won.

Ruthless rulers

Power went to some rulers' heads and they ruled as **tyrants**.

▲ Emperors wore purple clothes. It was **treason** for anyone other than the emperor to wear all-purple clothes.

▶ Tiberius tortured his enemies by breaking their legs. He had them thrown off cliffs where sailors waited with oars and boat hooks to finish them off.

◀ Valentinian I kept man-eating bears in a cage near his bedroom, and threw anyone who upset him inside it.

▶ Nero murdered his mother, two wives and his step-brother. He kept a pet glutton, a fat Egyptian slave who ate anything, including human flesh.

◀ Vitellius was a famous glutton himself. He ate four feasts a day, often making himself sick, so he could carry on eating.

Cruel Caligula

Caligula (37 – 41 CE) claimed to be a god, and had statues of himself placed in temples.

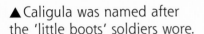
▲ Caligula was named after the 'little boots' soldiers wore.

▲ He loved dressing up and even robbed the grave of Alexander the Great so he could dress up in his armour!

Caligula organised huge killing spectacles between gladiators and animals in the Colosseum. In between fights, he fed the animals on prisoners because it was cheaper than buying meat!

The four-legged senator

Caligula had a favourite horse called Incitatus. He kept it in a marble stable and fed it from an ivory manger. He even made it a **senator**.

▲ Senators were threatened with death if they objected to the horse senator.

Glossary

anaesthetic	A drug that temporarily stops sensation or makes someone unconscious.
arson	The crime of deliberately setting fire to a building.
ballista	A giant catapult for throwing spears or stones.
cohort	A unit of 480 soldiers in a legion in the army.
Colosseum, the	A huge amphitheatre where games were held in Rome.
crucify	To be killed by being tied or nailed to a wooden cross.
decimation	A punishment by which one man in ten in a cohort was killed.
denarii	Roman coins.
farce	A light drama with slapstick comedy.
fort	An army post, occupied by soldiers.
forum	The market place in a Roman town or city.
fuller	A person whose job was to clean and prepare cloth.
garum	A salty sauce made from fish guts, used in cooking.
glutton	Someone who eats very greedily.
humours	Four substances in the human body that had to be kept in balance, according to Roman doctors: black bile, yellow bile, blood and phlegm.
leech	A blood-sucking worm.
litter	A portable bed or chair.
pater familias	Father, head of the family.
pumice stone	A piece of volcanic rock used to remove hair or rough skin.
resin	The gum from a tree.
senator	A member of the Senate, Rome's ruling body.
slander	To speak about someone in a damaging way.
strigil	A metal tool for scraping oils and dirt off the skin.
traitor	A person who commits treason.
treason	The crime of betraying a leader or country.
trident	A weapon with a forked end.
tyrant	A cruel and overbearing ruler.

Further Information

Books

Avoid Being a Roman Soldier (Danger Zone),
by David Stewart and David Antram,
Book House 2006

Men, Women and Children in Ancient Rome,
by Jane Bingham, Wayland 2007

The Rotten Romans (Horrible Histories),
by Terry Deary and Martin Brown,
Scholastic 2007

The Ruthless Romans (Horrible Histories),
by Terry Deary and Martin Brown,
Scholastic 2003

You Wouldn't Want to be a Roman Gladiator!,
by John Malam, Wayland 2000

Website

www.historyforkids.org/learn/Romans
www.roman-empire.net/children
www.bbc.co.uk/schools/romans

Places to visit

The Roman Legionary Museum,
Carleon, Wales
The Chedworth Roman Villa,
near Cirencester
The Roman baths, Bath

 # Author Note

The Romans really were a super people
and, even today, we are still using
many of their ideas and inventions.
However, Rome did decline and fall,
maybe because of some of the gruesome
truths in this book! I studied Latin at
school and learned lots about Roman
poetry and architecture, but I didn't
know then that the Romans had some
shocking habits, too!

Jillian Powell

# Index

# Answers

Page 6 What is it? A gladiator's helmet with face guard.

Page 7 True or false? True – maybe! The emperor did give a thumb sign: but experts are divided. Some think thumbs-up meant kill the criminal!

Page 8 What is it? Giant eggs and dolphins mounted on a pole were counted down to mark each completed lap in a chariot race.

Page 13 True or false? True. Boys offered their stubble as a sacrifice to the gods!

Page 17 What is it? A curse tablet. Romans placed curses like this in temples to bring their enemies bad luck.

Page 21 What is it? A soldier's money purse, worn as a bracelet to prevent theft.

Page 23 What is it? A bone ticket to freedom, won by a slave who had success as a gladiator.

Page 23 True or false? True. In a rebellion led by Spartacus the gladiator in 73 BCE, 6,000 slaves were crucified.

Page 25 True or false? True. Arcagathus arrived in Rome in 219 BCE. He got his nickname because so many of his patients died!

Page 25 What is it? A bone drill. Surgeons used bone drills to remove diseased bone or fragments of weapons.